Steamers of the Lakes vol2:
Coniston, Derwentwa̶t̶e̶r̶ ater
Robert Beale

Gondola, on Coniston.

© Robert Beale, 2011
First published in the United Kingdom, 2011,
by Stenlake Publishing Ltd.
www.stenlake.co.uk
01290 551122
ISBN 9781840335576

The publishers regret that they cannot supply
copies of any pictures featured in this book.

Thanks to Kim, Mum Dad, Ian McCrorie and also to John Newth.

A ticket for a cruise around Derwentwater estimated to be from the 1950s. The wooden launches that have been on the lake for many decades are currently going through a thorough overhaul. Some of them have been nearly completely rebuilt and look as if they are not even half their actual age! Hopefully they can continue to provide the service around the lake for another hundred years. As well as the main passenger operations, rowing boats have been for hire since tourists first arrived at Keswick, and more recently self-drive motor boats have been made available for hire as well.

Further Reading

The books listed below were used by the author during his research. None are available from Stenlake Publishing; please contact your local bookshop or reference library.

The Great Age of Steam on Windermere — G. H. Pattinson
The History of the Windermere Steamers — Robin Martakies
Lakeland Pleasure Craft — Ken Davies
The Coniston Railway — Michael Andrews and Geoff Holme
Steam Yacht Gondola — The National Trust

Introduction

The Lake District has many lakes, but none of them have had any passenger operations to match those of the four major lakes set out in these two books. On most of the other lakes, motor boats are not allowed access, but most allow the use of kayaks and canoes. Boating is not allowed on Thirlmere or Haweswater as these two are resevoirs. The four lakes; Windermere, Coniston, Ullswater and Derwentwater each provide an extensive timetable of operations throughout the summer months, and they all operate to a varying degree throughout the winter. Below is a list of ships who have operated on Coniston, Ullswater and Derwentwater, organised by the date the vessel arrived in the Lakes. For a fleet list of Windermere refer to Steamers of the Lakes Vol. 1.

Vessel Name	Built	Launch on Lake	Disposed	Area Operated
Queen of the Lakes	185X	1855	1855	Coniston
Enterprise	1859	1859	c.1877	Ullswater
Gondola	1859/1980	1859/1980	Still in Service	Coniston
Lady of the Lake	1877	1877	Still in Service	Ullswater
Raven	1889	1889	Still in Service	Ullswater
Waterlilly	1903	1903	c.2001	Derwentwater
May Queen	1904	1904	c.2001	Derwentwater
Iris	1908	1908	Currently Laid Up	Derwentwater
Lady of the Lake	1908	1908	1950	Coniston
Lady Derwentwater	1925	1925	Still in Service	Derwentwater
Annie Mellor	1935	1935	Still in Service	Derwentwater
Princess Margaret Rose	1938	1938	Still in Service	Derwentwater
Ruskin	1922	1991	Still in Service	Coniston
Ransome	1923	1994	2011	Coniston
Lakeland Mist	1954	1998	Still in Service	Derwentwater
Lady Dorothy	1967	2001	Still in Service	Ullswater
Lakeland Star	1978	2004	2011	Derwentwater
Lady Wakefield	1949	2005	Still in Service	Ullswater
Western Belle	1935	2010	Still in Service	Ullswater
Campbell	1976	2011	Still in Service	Coniston

Coniston Services

The mountains around Coniston are famous for the copper mines which are dotted around the fells. When the mines opened in the sixteenth century the copper ore was at first transported on horse and cart to Greenodd from where it was shipped away by sea. It was soon realised that the lake could be used to make the operation easier. The ore was taken to the head of the lake where it was loaded onto large barges which were towed behind a large rowing boat, probably with auxiliary sails, to Nibthwaite at the foot of the lake. At Nibthwaite it was transported by road to Greenodd, a considerably shorter distance. A small amount of gunpowder was transported in the opposite direction.

In 1855 the *Ulverston Advertiser* noted that from the 16th July a steam-propelled vessel would ply on Consiton Water. The article is worth quoting in length:

> A small steamer was yesterday launched at High Nibthwaite upon the glossy surface of Thurston or Coniston Lake, but whether for public or private use we are unable to ascertain. If the latter we doubt non the speculation will be a profitable one to the proprietor, and a great convenience to lake tourists. The romantic scenery of the neighbourhood and the salubrity of the district offer great attractions to pleasure seekers and tourists.

> The steamer is of the screw principle and came from Fleetwood. It was transported to Coniston Lake, and is, we understand the property of the Coniston Mining (Copper) Co. who intend running it for passengers and as a tug for the conveyance of ore down the lake.

A week later, on 19th July 1855, an amendment was made; it was stated that the steamer was in fact the property of a Mr. Sladen, and not that of the mining company.

On 26th July 1855 a timetable was published:-

> Coniston Lake Steamer – On and after Monday July 16th, the screw steamer *Queen of the Lakes* will ply from and too the Waterhead Inn, Coniston (weather Permitting) taking in passengers from both sides of the lake, via, Nibthaite and Lake Bank, as under:

> Down the lake – 09.30am, 12.15pm, and 4pm
> Up the lake – 10.40am, 1.30pm, and 5.30pm

> Fares from the round: First Class 1*s* 6*d*; Second Class 1*s*. Parties not returning charged same fare. Children under 12 half price. To Tourists: Parties travelling from Ambleside by the coach for Broughton will arrive in time for the boat leaving Waterhead at 12.15 and returning at 4 or 5.30pm. On Sundays the *Queen of the Lakes* will ply (weather permitting) as under:

> Down the lake – 09.30am, 1.30pm, and 5.30pm
> Up the lake – 10.45am, 3pm, and 7pm

> Fares as on Weekdays. The Steamer will call at Coniston Hall and Oxenhouses when required.

> James Sladen, Proprietor. Coniston Waterhead, July 1855.

As we can see the steamer had a number of calls to make at Waterhead, Coniston Hall, Oxenhouses, Nibthwaite and Lake Bank. The venture continued for about a month and then in the *Advertiser* on 16th August 1855:

> Steam boat on sale, the steamboat lately plying on Coniston Lake (but now discontinued) is, with all her materials to dispose of by private treaty. Apply to James Sladen, Hare Hill Mill, Littleborough, The Owner.

There is very little information about the actual vessel. The *Kendal Mercury* in July 1855 stated that the vessel had been designed to run on a canal. This leads one to believe that it may have been similar in appearance to many of the passenger vessels on the canals before the railways outmoded them. It is known that the *Queen of the Lakes* was very underpowered and may have plied on a waterway near Rochdale prior to being brought north. The venture had failed due to a lack of patronage. Coniston did not receive as much recognition as Windermere, the railway to that town arriving in 1847, bringing with it many tourists. In 1859 the Coniston branch line opened, connecting at Foxfield with the Furness Railway. If only Mr. Sladen had come four years later, he might have had the same success as the later boats which plied the lake.

When the Coniston Railway opened in 1859, no steam vessel had been operating on Coniston for nearly four years and the railway company commissioned a vessel to take tourists on Coniston in connection with the trains. The ship was designed by Douglas Hobson who had also designed several of the Windermere steamers and was built by Jones and Quiggin of Liverpool out of iron, at a cost of £1,100. She was transported to Coniston by rail, launched in October 1859, ran trials the following month and named the *Gondola*, with her passenger service starting the following month. Originally she had a railway boiler and no funnel. The steam was let out through an exhaust near the stern.

Her original timetable was to run a lake tour in the early afternoon, but to be on standby for request tours at either 11.30am or 4pm, if *"due notice be given"*. In her second season the 11.30am became a fixed trip in her schedule. In her first few years the *Gondola* was registered to a Mr. James Ramsden because the railway did not have powers to operate a steamboat service. In 1862 the Furness Railway took over the Coniston Railway, and in 1872 the 'Furness Railway (steamboats)' Act was introduced and the registration was transferred to the railway company.
Her vitals as built were:- 42 tons, 84 feet long, 14 feet 2 inches in the beam with a passenger capacity of 200 and an engine capable of providing her with 14hp.

She was an immediate success and passenger figures rose every year until in 1897 she carried 14,264 passengers. This was not beaten again until 1980 when 22,445 were carried. Inside *Gondola* was the pinnacle of luxury with her dark red seating complete with cushions you could sink into, surrounded with white and gold panelling. After a short while, the exhaust system was found to be uneconomical, so a funnel was put in place instead of a stern pipe. Not only did this work but performance was improved as well. The Furness Railway continued to run the *Gondola* with much success until 1908 when the *Lady of the Lake* was launched, and the *Gondola* was placed in reserve. The *Lady of the Lake* was built by the Furness Railway Company to take over the Coniston lake service from the 50 year old *Gondola*. Plans were laid down in 1907 with a Southampton based firm – J & I Thornycroft. She was pieced together at Waterhead and when launched she was 76 tons, 92 feet long, 15.1 feet wide and with a draught of 4 feet. She had a canoe shaped bow, not unlike the *Tern* which still plies on Windermere.

This set-up didn't last long, and the *Gondola* was brought back into service due to excessive demand, to run a limited secondary service to the *Lady of the Lake*. With the advent of The First World War in 1914 the two ships were taken out of service for the duration. After the war the *Lady of the Lake* more than catered for the number of passengers on Coniston, many of them coming as part of a circular tour operated by the railway company.

Along with the *Gondola* she was laid up in 1939 upon the outbreak of the Second World War. Unfortunately, due to lack of post-war demand she was scrapped in 1946.

The outbreak of the Second World War led to the withdrawal of both steamers, the *Gondola* in 1936 and the *Lady of the Lake* in 1939. The *Gondola* was sold. Her engine went to a local sawmill and she was converted to a houseboat in 1946/47 and moored at the southeastern corner of Coniston. By this time she had already completed 80 years in service. For these 80 years she only had three permanent masters. The first was Captain Anderson who had seen service in Arctic expeditions, then Felix Hamil served with her for 50 years, before Captain Priss took over upon his retiral. In 1963 she was badly damaged in a winter storm and ended up ashore near Water Park in a very bad way. The story continues in 1966 when Mr. Arthur Hatton acquired her and moved her to a more secluded location, where she was sunk in order to preserve her hull. Here she stayed for twelve more years until 1978 when the National Trust bought her, and started making plans for re-floating, which was completed the same year. They took her to Coniston Hall, and then on to Vickers Shipyard at Barrow. Anything that could be saved from the grand old lady was. She was re-built during 1979 using original plans obtained from the London Science Museum and on 25th March 1980 she was re-launched, commencing passenger service on the 24th June that same year. During her first year back in service she was operated by Sealink, who also operated the steamers on Windermere, on behalf of the National Trust. Subsequently the National Trust assumed full responsibility for the running of the vessel.

For the next twelve years *Gondola* had the run of the lake doing a number of trips daily between Coniston, Lake Bank, and later Monk Coniston. In 1992 Coniston Ferry Services, founded by Gordon and Margaret Hall, started operations between Coniston, Brantwood and Monk Coniston using a launch named the *Ruskin* which was built in 1922 for the Chester Boat Company as the *Raglan II*. She worked on the River Dee for this company until the outbreak of the Second World War, when she was requisitioned by the admiralty for use as a minesweeper and renamed HMS *Ariel*, her wooden hull being an advantage in this role. After her war service she returned to the River Dee in 1946 and continued to be owned by the Chester Boat Company until it was taken over in 1982 by Bithells Boats. Coniston Ferry Services purchased her in 1991, renamed her, and altered her to the traditional Lakeland Style, with open bow and covered aft accommodation.

The new operation was more successful than first anticipated, and so to accommodate the extra trade the launch *Iris* was chartered from Derwentwater in 1994. A year later a new vessel, the *Ransome*, was introduced which allowed the *Iris* to return north to Derwentwater. Built in 1923 as the *Monarch I* at Portsmouth, the *Ransome* , like her future sister. was requisitioned by the admiralty for the duration of the Second World War. She was used as a harbour launch at Portsmouth, and later on the Thames. After the war and back doing passenger services she served for twenty years working out of Windsor, and after a brief stint elsewhere, came to Coniston in 1994. Renamed the *Ransome* she allowed the company to expand the cruises offered, working with the *Ruskin*. Both vessels were powered by diesel engines when they arrived at Coniston, and operated as such until 1995 when they were converted to solar-electric propulsion. More piers were added to the timetable including Waterhead, Lake Bank, Sunny Bank, Torver and Water Park.

In 2008 the company changed hands, and the new owners have upgraded the fleet, withdrawing *Ransome*. *Ransome* spent the beginning of 2011 laid up until she was disposed of in May. Meanwhile a new vessel was launched on the lake ready to enter service in the last week of May. *Campbell* was built in 1976, originally for use as one of the Starcross ferries operating from Exmouth to Starcross, and named *Exonia (II)*. She operated the ferry for various owners until D & P Faithful bought her for use on Portsmouth Harbour tours in 1999. *Exonia (II)* was moved to a local boatyard near Hawkshead in late 2010 to be refurbished, re–engined and made ready for service on Coniston Water. Renamed *Campbell* she now sails daily. *Campbell* is diesel powered, *Ruskin* is electric and *Gondola* is steam. Three boats each with a different means of power!

The *Gondola* was 150 years old in 2009 making her the second oldest passenger carrying vessel anywhere in the world in regular use (depending on whether you count from her original launch date, or her newer one!). Let's hope she can manage another 150 years.

A timeless picture, *Gondola* is shown here arriving at Pier Cottage in the northern reaches of Coniston Water. Pier Cottage has been the traditional home of the *Gondola* since her original launch in 1859. Her first master was a man named Captain Anderson, but her second master was Felix Hamil. He was master of the vessel for over 50 years, and he was never far from the *Gondola*. He used to live in the cottage overlooking his vessel with his nine children! When the *Lady of the Lake* came in 1908 Felix took over the new craft, whilst a Captain Priss took on the *Gondola*.

Unfortunately no pictures have surfaced of the first steamer on Coniston, the *Queen of the Lakes* which operated in 1855, but we are informed that she was reminiscent of a canal boat. *Gondola* was built by Jones and Quiggin of Liverpool and launched in December 1859 to operate in conjunction with the newly formed Coniston Railway which joined the Furness Railway at Foxfield. Like most other lake steamers in the area she was transported in sections by rail as close to her launch site as possible, then horses completed the transfer. *Gondola*'s first season was 1860 when she was operated by the Coniston Railway. This set-up lasted for three years until the Furness Railway took over the railway in 1862. Unlike the majority of steam ships, she was built with a locomotive boiler, a feature which has been retained even after her rebuild and can be seen today. This picture shows her as built with no funnel and an exhaust system instead. She didn't last long without a funnel, and as fumes started to become a problem a tall, heavily raked funnel was added. The picture is from the *Illustrated London News* which recorded the vessel's launch. Note how she is steered with a tiller.

Gondola was the epitome of luxury and sported a first class saloon set forward, well away from the engine. Her third class saloon was a little more spartan but still was a very comfortable area. After the addition of her funnel she looked the part and continued to operate from Coniston Pier to Lake Bank at the southern end of the lake. A trip on the *Gondola* was part of many of the Lakeland tours operated by the railway companies. These involved trains, coaches and steamer trips on Coniston and Windermere and to a lesser extent Ullswater. *Gondola* is depicted here with her funnel. The engine room is visible and open. allowing tourists to watch the engineer at work. Originally she was coal-fired, but in 2008 the National Trust started to use blazer logs which burn more efficiently than coals, as well as being better for the environment.

The overnight berth for the steamers of the Furness Railway was at the boathouse just north of the main pier which is now known as Coniston Landing Stage. The most famous captain of the *Gondola* was Captain Hamill. He lived with his ten children in the boathouse and was master of both vessels for over 50 years. He had spent time at sea prior to coming to the lake. The boathouse is still used today and it is where the *Gondola, Ruskin* and *Campbell* are all kept and maintained during the winter.

After the introduction of the *Lady of the Lake*, *Gondola* was withdrawn from service, but due to public outcry this didn't last long and she was soon running a back-up schedule. Over 60 years after the withdrawal of the *Lady of the Lake*, *Gondola* is still steaming her way up and down the lake. Surely part of her continued appeal is that *Gondola* is the only daily steam-powered service operating on the lakes. Steam trains are commonplace but a steam boat of *Gondola*'s size is a rare find indeed. This picture shows her as she looks today steaming elegantly towards the pier at Coniston Boating Centre.

When *Gondola* was rebuilt, it was to the original specifications as laid out in the plans. The plans for the boiler were actually borrowed from the Science Museum and today it is a pleasure to watch the engineer throw the blazer logs into the furnace. Whilst on board if one can tear oneself away from the magnificent scenery which inspired John Ruskin, then to relax in the saloons is well worth the fare alone. The saloon is decorated in the red and gold of the first class lounge and harks back to the long-gone Victorian age of excess when nothing seemed impossible. The vessel slices through the water so smoothly, and the machinery works so quietly that the noise and vibrations are only noticed by their absence.

Lady of the Lake was launched in 1908. She was built for the increase in trade on Coniston and was a larger vessel than her fleetmate, the *Gondola*. She traded alone for a number of seasons, but pretty soon the *Gondola* was running alongside her as demand had increased beyond expectations. The First World War saw both vessels being withdrawn from service, but *Lady of the Lake* restarted again after the war and remained in service until 1939. *Lady of the Lake* is shown here at the southern end of the lake, by Lake Bank Jetty. Note the canoe-shaped bow. *Tern* on Windermere has a similar style bow, and was built for the same company, the Furness Railway.

As with the *Gondola*, and all the steamers on Windermere, ownership of the *Lady of the Lake* transferred to the London Midland & Scottish Railway Company in 1923. With that came new navy blue uniforms, brass buttons and a peaked cap. Her first master was Felix Hamill who had been captain of the *Gondola* for many years previously. A trip on *Lady of the Lake* was part of a number of tours offered by the railway company. The most popular was the Inner Circle which involved a steamer from Fleetwood to Barrow, train to Greenodd, horse-drawn carriage to Lake Bank and then steamer to Waterhead. From there the tourist would travel by train back to Barrow, and steamer to Fleetwood.

Lake Bank Jetty again is the setting for this picture of *Lady of the Lake*. She was converted from steam to diesel by the LMS and continued in service until the outbreak of the Second World War in 1939 when she was withdrawn, three years after her companion vessel, *Gondola*. *Lady of the Lake* was never to sail again with passengers. She was scrapped in 1950. Lake Bank Pier is still in use today, although by the Coniston Launches. *Gondola* has landed there recently and it is hoped that regular services will operate again. Interesting to note is the structure which stands on the pier which is a typical Furness Railway style building. Note the man at the stern of the vessel with his legs hanging over the sides.

Lady of the Lake is about to pick up a heavy load at Lake Bank Jetty here. The tourists are probably doing one of the many tours offered by the railway companies which we mentioned earlier. Just to the right of the picture is the lake's outflow, the River Crake, which flows out into the River Leven at Greenodd and then out into Morecambe Bay. In the old days flooding was a regular occurrence during the late summer, usually August. Heavy rains combined with the silting up of the river would result in the submerging of the piers, meaning the steamers could not sail. Thankfully the river was subsequently dredged allowing the river to drain faster.

Ruskin was the first vessel operated by the Coniston Launch Company. She was built in 1922 as the *Raglan II* at Chester to operate as a pleasure craft on the Dee Estuary. She served the admiralty as a minesweeper during the Second World War and after operating for a number of pleasure companies, she ended up at Coniston in 1992. Hew new owners renovated her and made her profile match that of the traditional "Lakeland style" launch, a covered stern with an open bow. She was so successful that in 1994 she was joined by the *Iris*, as launch from Derwentwater. *Ruskin* operates from Coniston Boating Centre to Waterhead, Torver and Brantwood all year round, and in summer also serves Lake Bank, Sunny Bank and Water Park.

When she was brought to Coniston, *Ruskin* was diesel-powered. In 2005 the Coniston Launch Company "went green" and converted her and her fleet mate, *Ransome* to solar-electric power. They both received an electric motor and solar panels on the roof of the saloon. Power is stored in batteries and if the sun does not shine enough to charge the batteries, an overnight charge ensures the boat won't run out of power during a trip! The electric propulsion ensures a smooth and quiet run on the lake.

In 1994 the Coniston Launch Company were operating the *Ruskin* and the chartered *Iris*. To let the *Iris* return to Derwentwater, the company located a new vessel for the lake. *Ransome* was delivered to Coniston in 1994. She had been built at Portsmouth in 1923 and like her future stablemate, also served the admiralty during the Second World War. She remained at Portsmouth for most of this, as a harbour launch. After ending the war on the Thames, she moved to Windsor and then Shepperton. After her delivery to Coniston in 1994 she was refurbished and converted to a more traditional look, ready to enter service in 1995. *Ransome* is seen here at Coniston Boating Centre ready for a trip around the Northern Service to Waterhead, Torver and Brantwood.

Like the *Ruskin*, the *Ransome* was converted to electric propulsion in 2005. In this picture the *Gondola* and the *Ransome* are shown passing each other during the 2010 season, which was also *Ransome*'s last season. Although the companies operate rival services, the competition is friendly. A trip on *Gondola* is to gain a first-hand experience of how the first class Victorians travelled, and a trip on *Ruskin* or *Campbell* is to travel on historical boats with innovative propulsion systems. The Coniston Launches also serve more piers enabling walkers to get off at one pier, and rejoin the vessel at another. Both companies operate special cruises about the history of the lake, or themed trips about Swallows and Amazons.

Derwentwater

Derwentwater is situated in the northern Lake District near Keswick. It has a passenger launch service operating throughout the summer and on a limited basis in winter. There is a long history of passenger operations on the lake stretching back over a century. The railway from Penrith reached Keswick in 1865 and with that the area was easily opened up to tourists. It was due to this increase that by 1910 there were eight operators offering cruises on the lake. Six of these operators were private families, and the other two were hotels, the Derwentwater Hotel and the Lodore Hotel. The latter used to run electric launches whose batteries were charged up using power harnessed from the majestic Lodore waterfalls behind the hotel. The competition was rife on the foreshore where the different operators were clamouring for the business of the tourists and disturbances were not uncommon. Two of the earliest known pleasure boats on the lake were the *Lorna Doone*, a coal-fired steamer capable of carrying up to 53 passengers and the *Derwent*, another steamer, capable of carrying 23 passenger. The Derwent Launch and Motor Company was formed prior to 1916 and they operated mainly between Lodore and Portinscale. *Iris* was built in 1908 on Windermere. Along with the *May Queen* she was one of the launches used by the Lodore Hotel to convey guests between Portinscale and the hotel. She has changed owners over the years and now operates for the Keswick Launch Company and has been converted to diesel. In the 1990s she spent a season on Coniston before they got the *Ransome*.

1933 was the year the Keswick-on-Derwentwater Launch Company Limited (known as Keswick Launch Company) was formed by the amalgamation of the boatmen, who previously had been in fierce competition with each other. It is this company which has become the sole operator of pleasure cruises on the lake today. The Keswick Launch Company operates between seven landing stages around the lake and with the exception of one all their launches are over seventy years old. Their fleet originally consisted of the small wooden launches *Waterlilly*, *May Queen*, *Iris*, *Annie Mellor*, *Lady Derwentwater* and *Princess Margaret Rose*. In 1998 they acquired a waterbus from Loch Lomond, their first vessel not to be made of wood. Even so, *Lakeland Mist* has been well fitted out so she blends in and looks like a classic launch. In 2004 the catamaran *Twin Star II* was purchased, re-named *Lakeland Star*, and placed in service. Unfortunately she had a deeper draught than the other vessels, and was not practical in the shallow bays of the lake, and had to be sold. *Waterlilly* and *May Queen* have now been withdrawn and the *Iris* is currently laid up.

Lakeland Mist is shown here at Hawes End landing stage on Derwentwater on the first run of the day around the lake during one of the hardest winters to affect the Lakes in recent years. Services on Derwentwater run all year round, although during the winter the services are restricted. *Lakeland Mist* is very similar to the *Miss Cumbria* vessels on Windermere, and her hull is made of steel which can easily withstand the plunging temperatures of a Lakeland winter better than the wooden launches. This enables a winter service to be carried out. The launches are overhauled thoroughly at a slipway on Isthmus Bay not far from the main landing stages. Currently there are four launches ready for service whilst another two are laid up at the time of writing.

Derwentwater, which is located just south of the town of Keswick is regarded by many as the most beautiful of the English Lakes and long been a draw for tourists. The lake has probably been used for many centuries for the transport of material from the local mines. There has never been a large steamer service to rival that of the other lakes, but small pleasure launches started operating in the early years of the twentieth century and one of the first was owned by the Lodore Hotel, who operated an electric launch to convey tourists between the hotel and the town. This picture shows one of the hotel's launches at the Keswick landing stage.

May Queen is seen here on the approach to one of the landing stages at Derwentwater. *May Queen* was built in 1904 and she was one of the launches used by the Lodore Hotel to convey guests between Portinscale and the Lodore hotel. She was withdrawn from service after over 90 years of service on the lake. The service today is very popular with walkers using the Hawes End, and both the Brandelhow landing stages to provide easy access to the hill of Cat bells. The view from the summit of Cat bells is regarded by many to be one of the finest in the whole of the Lake District.

The same boat as in the last picture is pictured here, this time in front of the Lodore Hotel. One of the launches the hotel used was the *Iris*, built on Windermere in 1908. The Keswick-on-Derwentwater Launch Company came into being in 1933 and started to offer an extensive service on the lake calling at six jetties in both clockwise, and anti-clockwise directions. *Annie Mellor* was originally a houseboat on Windermere. but was moved to Derwentwater and converted to passenger use. By the early sixties the company had six boats in operation: *Waterlily*, *Iris*, *May Queen*, *Lady Derwentwater*, *Annie Mellor* and *Princess Margaret Rose*.

A seventh scheduled call was added to the route, at Nichol End, very close to the village of Portinscale. Currently the company offer cruises all year round, although in the quietest time of year they only operate at weekends. Evening cruises, walkers' specials and Santa cruises are also offered. Derwentwater has more traditional wooden launches for public use than any other lake, and is well worth a visit. Rowing boats are available here as well and these are just as well-maintained as the launches. Pictured at the Keswick Landing Stage are *Annie Mellor*, *May Queen*, *Princess Margaret Rose*, *Waterlilly* and *Lady Derwentwater*.

The first new vessel for the company for over fifty years was *Lakeland Mist*. Built in 1954 as the *Prinses Juliana* in Amsterdam, she operated on the canals there before moving to Loch Lomond. At Loch Lomond she operated for Cruise Loch Lomond from their base in Tarbet under her new name of *Lomond Mist*. In 1998 she was sold for use on Derwentwater and moved to the lake in April. In 2004 they took delivery of another new boat, a catamaran from the River Thames called *Twin Star II* which was built in 1978. Like many secondhand lake vessels she was sailed up the coast to Whitehaven and then transferred to the lake by lorry. The vessel was renamed *Lakeland Star* and entered service. *Lakeland Star* had a deeper draught than the wooden launches, and this meant that when the lake was low she couldn't berth at some of the jetties. This picture shows *Annie Mellor* and *Lakeland Mist* on Derwentwater in 2010. *Lakeland Star* can be seen on the slipway, half hidden by the trees across the bay, prior to her sale in March 2011 to the River Dart.

Ullswater Services

Ullswater is situated in the eastern Lake District, and is the second longest of the lakes. At eight miles long it is close behind Windermere, and longer than Coniston's five and a half miles. Unlike these, Ullswater has no rail links, and has never developed to such an extent. As a result a sail along the waters of Ullswater is a different experience altogether.

There is a reference in an old guidebook to a small iron paddle steamer which operated between Pooley Bridge and Patterdale to transport goods for the lead and slate mines as early as 1849 but no other evidence apart from this reference exists.

The first vessel we are sure operated on the lake was the *Enterprise*. The Ullswater Steam Navigation Company was formed in 1855 with the aim of introducing steam navigation to the lake. In 1859 they launched the little wooden paddle steamer *Enterprise* which was built locally at Pooley Bridge and launched in August to serve the village of Howtown halfway along the southern shore, and Patterdale at the head of the lake. At Patterdale there were slate and lead mine workings, and it was for these that the small steamer was primarily built to serve. The local paper was there to record the event.

> Several hundreds of spectators assembled to witness an operation novel to the inhabitants of these dales, the inland navigation of Ullswater having hitherto been restricted to skiffs and oar boats and a light yacht or two.

A few months later the same paper, the *Carlisle Patriot*, recorded:

> A commodious vessel with accommodation of a superior character. She sails swiftly and steadily, and although the arrangements for landing passengers and the discipline of the crew are not yet completed, yet, in the course of a lifetime, and with little experience of two or three more trips, there can be no doubt that she will prove another great source of attraction to this beautiful location.

Not much is known about her at all, but a number of stories relating to her have lasted through time. One of *Enterprise*'s captains was a Kendal man called Thomas Metcalfe Thompson. He had spent his young adulthood at sea, and upon returning had been the captain of the *Swan* (I) (1869) on Windermere. He transferred to Ullswater in the early 1870s, and met with Captain Cornett, the previous captain of the *Enterprise*. Captain Cornett told him of a previous captain who used to play a trick on the tourists. As the vessel sailed past Kailpot Crag in central Ullswater he would say it was a lucky omen to be able to throw a silver piece into a hole in the rock on the island. He would then watch with glee as the silver piled up on the island and return later to collect it!

In the 1860s the company had difficulty maintaining access to landings and rights to sail. This ended up in court cases, one even going as far as the House of Lords. It is not known exactly when *Enterprise* was withdrawn from service but it was definitely after 1877, as it is known that the *Lady of the Lake* had to assist her when some hay clogged up her paddle wheels. It is likely that the *Lady of the Lake* was her replacement, and the two ran together only for a short while until the newer vessel was approved by the company as suitable.

Lady of the Lake was a screw steamer designed by Mr. Douglas Hebson from Penrith and built built by T.B. Seath & Co of Rutherglen. She was launched on 26th June 1877 and is still in service today. Depending on whether you class the Coniston *Gondola* as older, *Lady of the Lake* is the third oldest passenger vessel in regular use anywhere in the world. As far as the author can ascertain the only older (regular working) vessels are the *Skibladner*, a paddler which survives in Norway, her maiden voyage occurring in 1856, and the *Enköping* which works in Sweden and was launched in 1868.

The Ullswater Steam Navigation Company had gained a subsidy from the Royal Mail to carry the mails along the lake, so the *Lady of the Lake* was known as a Royal Mail Steam Ship. She has had an interesting career, including a fire and sinking twice, and still trades daily in the summer. In 1881 *Lady of the Lake* sank at her moorings, and could not be raised for some weeks due to a spate of bad weather. Luckily her owners were swift with her salvage when the weather had abated, and a team of divers from Liverpool managed to raise her and she was pressed back into service relatively quickly. Originally she was powered by a four cylinder steam engine which pushed her along at a respectable 12 knots. In 1888 *Lady of the Lake* broke down and had to spend a number of weeks out of service. It was due to this one of the directors, Thomas Cook suggested that a new vessel should be added to complement the *Lady of the Lake*'s sailings.

Raven was another product of T.B. Seath & Co, and was launched on 16th July 1889. Like her sister before, she was totally built at Rutherglen on the Clyde, then dismantled and taken by train to Penrith and coach in sections to Pooley Bridge where she was re-assembled. She is a larger vessel than her sister but was originally powered by the same type of steam engine. 1895 was a proud year for the new vessel as she carried the Crown Prince of Germany along the lake when he was a guest of Lord Lonsdale of Lowther Castle. In 1900 the company was renamed the Ullswater Navigation & Transit Company and in 1906 a third vessel was looked at with the prospect of joining the fleet. The vessel was called *Osprey*, but instead of purchasing her, the company instead decided to re-boiler the *Lady of the Lake*. In 1904 the company name was officially changed to the Ullswater Navigation and Transit Company. The new company produced some lovely guidebooks about the lake and surrounding area, which are very sought after today. As well as describing the lake, they also showed the tourist some easy walks and other things to do whilst on holiday in the area.

In 1935 both ships were converted from steam to oil and they each had new engines and their original funnels replaced with new motor ship style ones. During the Second World War both ships were laid up. The *Lady of the Lake* re-entered service in 1947 and served alone for a number of years until the *Raven* joined her again. It was around this time that the ships were repainted in the colours of the Cunard ship *Caronia* (1948-1974), pale green hull with red funnels topped with black. The next major event in the story of these boats was in 1950 when the *Lady of the Lake* sank again, this time at Pooley Bridge. She was under water for a while, but was raised and again re-entered service looking brand new after repairs. The steamer company changed hands in 1954 as Sir Wavell Wakefield of Kendal purchased a majority share in the company when he heard the services on the lake were to be stopped. He later went on to purchase the Ravenglass and Eskdale Railway to prevent its closure as well.

In the meantime the steamer fleet on Windermere had been updated and one vessel was lying at Lakeside up for sale. *Cygnet* had been built in 1879 for the Furness Railway. When she was withdrawn from service, she was sold to Lord Wakefield who was going to operate her under the Ullswater Steam Navigation Company flag. In anticipation of the move she received a new paint job and new funnel. As it happened she never left Windermere and was instead converted into a houseboat, later being scrapped in 1964.

By the late 1950s *Raven*'s engines were in need of replacement, and in 1964 she received a pair of Thorneycroft engines. It was also at this time when the wheelhouse of *Raven* was moved forward. By far the most destructive incident occurred in 1965 when *Lady of the Lake* was gutted by fire. She was on the slipway at Waterside near Pooley Bridge when one of the sheds went up in flames. She was close enough to be damaged and remained out of commission until 1978 when she was re launched with two new Kelvin engines. In 2004 *Raven* was re-engined with Cummins engines. *Lady of the Lake* followed in 2005. Things settled down then for the sisters and they continue to provide the seasonal service today.

In 2001 winter sailings were introduced with the acquisition of the *Lady Dorothy*. *Lady Dorothy* was built in 1967 and served in the Channel Islands sailing between Guernsey and Herm. In her later years she was used as an overflow vessel and was sold to Ullswater in 2001. She was restored by a local boat builder and now keeps the service running throughout the year.

Another new vessel joined the fleet in 2005. *Lady Wakefield* was built in 1949 for the River Dart Steamboat Company which operated cruises between Totnes and Dartmouth and many places in between. She was originally named *Berry Castle* (III). The company started to notice a drop in trade so in 1972 *Berry Castle* (III) was sold to a company which planned to use her as a dive boat in Honduras. This project fell through and she moved on to Fareham and then Rochester on the Medway where she was renamed *Golden Cormorant*. Eventually in 1977 she found her way home to the Dart under the flag of the Dart Pleasure Craft Company who had replaced the River Dart Steamboat Company as the lead operator on the river. They named her *Totnes Castle* (III) and continued to use her out of Plymouth, after they purchased the Millbrook Steamboat & Trading Company, until 1985 when the company stopped operating in the Plymouth area. Plymouth Boat Cruises picked her up and operated her under the same name until 2005 when she was transferred to Ullswater having sailed up the coast to Whitehaven from where she was transported by lorry to the lake to begin a two year refurbishment. In 2006 her Gardner engines were refurbished, and she entered service the following year.

The newest ship on Ullswater is the *Western Belle*. She was built in Great Yarmouth in 1935 for the Millbrook Steam Boat & Trading Company and was used on the Plymouth to Millbrook ferry as well as excursions covering the Rivers Tamar and Yealm. She continued right through the Second World War and apart from a brief charter to British Railways on the River Dart in 1955 she continued to operate the Millbrook ferry up until 1985 when the Millbrook Company, now owned by the Dart Pleasure Craft Company, ceased trading in the Plymouth area. They moved her to the

River Dart where she operated until 2000. In this year she was sold to Chris Cruises who used her for charters on the River Thames.

After her sale in 2008 to the Ullswater Navigation & Transit Company she sailed under her own power to Maryport where she was laid up for a year prior being moved to the Mersey for a refit before her move, by lorry, to Ullswater in July 2010. After being towed by *Lady Dorothy* to the slip, she underwent final modifications and entered service in late 2010.

The timetables on the lake have varied greatly over the past few years with extra boats being added to the fleet. The basic service is from Pooley Bridge to Glenridding via Howtown and vice-versa but half lake cruises are offered, and the service is maintained through the winter every day apart from Christmas Eve and Christmas Day. The ships are well maintained and have heated accommodation perfect for a winter cruise. In many people's opinion the Lakes are at their best on a crisp cold day in early January, sailing down the glassy waters with snow dusting the tops of the fells.

The three reaches of Ullswater, Patterdale Pier is located at the bottom right of the picture on the northern shore (nearest the camera). Coaches connected at Patterdale from Windermere, Troutbeck (north) and Ambleside with the steamers which would leave here on the way via Howtown to Pooley Bridge. Howtown is situated on the southern (right hand side) where the lake swings north east (left on the picture). Pooley Bridge and the River Eamont lie at the furthest point of Ullswater from the camera. Here coaches met each steamer and conveyed through passengers to Penrith and the rail network.

There is a reference to a small paddle steamer operating on the lake as early as 1849 in an old guidebook, but no other evidence has come to light to support this. The first steamer we are sure of to operate on Ullswater was the locally built wooden paddle steamer *Enterprise* which was launched in 1859. Unfortunately no pictures have surfaced of this vessel. She is believed to have lasted in service until not long after the *Lady of the Lake* entered service in 1877. We know this because shortly after *Lady of the Lake* entered service she had to tow the *Enterprise* to shallower waters after her paddles became clogged with hay. The *Enterprise* was built to serve Howtown and Patterdale from Pooley Bridge. This picture shows Pooley Bridge Pier, at the eastern end of the lake where it drains into the River Eamont which then joins the River Eden and flows out into the Solway Firth near Carlisle. The steamer at the pier is the *Lady of the Lake* after her conversion to motor ship in the 1930s.

After travelling west for nearly half an hour the little steamer would enter a bay (known as Howtown Wyke), approximately halfway along the southern edge of the lake. The pier there served the small village of Howtown and the settlements in the surrounding valleys of Martindale and Boredale. The Ullswater steamers were a vital link in the early days, as the roads around the lake were rather primitive. The boats would have carried everything from parcels and mail to tourists, and everything in between. In the early guide books published by the Ullswater Steam Navigation Company a number of walks were advertised from this pier. Today the walks are still advertised, the most popular one involving a steamer trip to Howtown and then the walk along the shoreline to Glenridding. Even at the most remote pier on the lake, rowing boats were still available.

At the head of the lake is the pier which serves the largest settlement. Originally known as Patterdale Pier, it was built to serve the small villages of Glenridding and Patterdale along with the extensive mine workings that litter the fells in the locality. The village of Patterdale is actually half a mile from the lake. The magnificent Ullswater Hotel was built nearby and there was a pier in the hotel grounds. Several hundred yards south along the shoreline, and out of the hotel's grounds is the pier used today, known as Glenridding Pier. The postcard portrays the *Raven* at the hotel pier with rowing boats at the hotel, and an old motor car at the head of the pier.

Lady of the Lake was launched on 26th June 1877 and had been built by T.B. Seath & Co of Rutherglen who produced many fine ships for inland waters. As well as *Lady of the Lake* and *Raven* on Ullswater, they built, for service in the Lakes, *Raven*, *Esperance*, *Swift*, *Britannia* and *Swan* (I) for Windermere. *Lady of the Lake* was transported by rail to Penrith in sections, and then on to the lake where she was reconstructed. As built she had ten windows and this postcard shows her in her original condition, leaving Howtown. She is 110 feet long and 15 feet wide. She draws 4 feet and weighs in at 43 tonnes. She was a Royal Mail Steam Ship, contracted to carry the mails along the lake. Royal Mail contracts were advantageous to any company which could secure them. Not only did it mean a subsidy, but it also allowed the use of Royal in the name of the ship which would be a boost to any venture.

This picture shows an altered *Lady of the Lake* with an extended saloon which now sports twelve windows and a wheelhouse. Note how the bridge position has moved forward of the funnel. In 1881 *Lady of the Lake* sank at her moorings, but was rescued by a team of divers from Liverpool. This was the first of a series of unfortunate events to befall this ship. After her raising, she entered service again, and soon had a fleet mate, the *Raven*. *Lady of the Lake* was converted from steam power to diesel in 1935 and she received a pair of Crossley engines. She also gained a new funnel.

In one day a tourist could travel from as far as Fleetwood or Leeds and see the sights of the Lakes and be home the same day. *Lady of the Lake* is seen here approaching Patterdale, extremely full, possibly as part of a tour. The guidebook produced by the steamer company in the 1920s describes a number of these tours. One could catch the train from Penrith to Troutbeck (on the line to Keswick), then go by coach to Patterdale, take the steamer to Pooley Bridge and coach back to Penrith. Another trip involved the train from Penrith to Windermere via Kendal, coach over the famous Kirkstone Pass to Ullswater, thence by steamer to Pooley Bridge and coach to Penrith. There are six tours advertised in the guide, but if one studied the timetable hard enough, there were many more possibilities.

Both *Lady of the Lake* and the *Raven* underwent conversion to diesel propulsion in the 1930s. With this they also both received new funnels and are seen here together at Pooley Bridge. When relaunched *Lady of the Lake* had yet another window arrangement, this time eight windows and a canvas roof to cover the stern of the vessel. *Lady of the Lake* is on the south (left) side of the pier, whilst *Raven* sits closer to the camera. During the Second World War, *Lady of the Lake* remained on the slip at Waterside Farm, leaving the *Raven* to carry on alone until 1947. Two decades after her conversion to diesel *Lady of the Lake* had another catastrophe and sank again at Pooley Bridge in September 1950.

Lady of the Lake is featured again, this time at Pooley Bridge in 1965. It was later this year that she was to be damaged by fire while on the slip at Eusemere, near Pooley Bridge. The shed nearest her caught fire and *Lady of the Lake* was close enough to sustain substantial damage. This resulted in her being out of service until 1978. When relaunched it was with her second set of new engines. She received Kelvin engines to replace her forty year old Crossleys. Her Kelvin engines lasted until 2005 when she was again re-engined.

Lady of the Lake's new Cummings engines provide her power today, pushing her through the water at ten knots with a passenger complement of 220. At 134 years old [in 2011] this ship is one of the oldest passenger vessels in regular working service on the planet. The fresh water goes a long way to preserving the Lake District fleet, but the amount of care that is lavished on these vessels keeps them in immaculate condition year in, year out. This photograph shows the grand old *Lady of the Lake* after her 1978 rebuild.

A company image of *Raven* in her original build. *Raven*, is currently the longest vessel on Ullswater and at 20 tonnes heavier is considerably larger than *Lady of the Lake*. Lady of the Lake and Raven are the oldest working ships in Britain. The author can only find two older ships in regular service in the world, PS *Skibladner* (1856) which operates on Lake Mjøsa in Norway, and MV *Enköping* (1868) the oldest passenger ship on Lloyds Registry which is operated on charter sailings around the Stockholm archipeligo in Sweden.

A crowded *Raven* departs from Patterdale Pier on a trip up the lake. See how every person on board the boat has a hat on! The bridge, still situated at the after end of the vessel is still an open one, and only has a canvas surround to protect the crew from the weather, a lovely prospect in the middle of summer, but even the best summer has wind and rain. Like her sister she was converted from steam in 1935. She received a pair of eight cylinder oil engines from the National Gas and Oil Engine Company. Unlike her stablemate, *Raven* has never suffered any major problems in her career. During the Second World War she was laid up, but re-entered service for the 1946 season.

Raven is passing Kail Pot Crag in this view from the late nineteenth century. Once past this rocky promontory, the steamer would turn into Howtown Wyke, and berth at Howtown Pier. Note the bridge is still of the open type, and situated behind the funnel which must have caused some difficulty when looking forward.

Raven is seen here as altered to motor ship, but with her wheelhouse still in its original position. The wheelhouse was moved forward in the sixties, not long after she was re-engined for the second time. In the winter of 1964/65 she received a pair of Thorneycroft diesel engines which lasted her up until 2004 when she received a pair of Cummings. These push her through the water at ten knots with a passenger complement of 246.

Raven is pictured here after her wheelhouse was moved forward. She still has it in this position today. The moving of the wheelhouse allowed a roof to be more aesthetically added to the ship, and makes navigation of the ship easier. There is only one large ship in the Lake District fleet which maintains her wheelhouse at the rear of the vessel, and this is the *Gondola* on Coniston. (Picture Credit John Newth)

Above: Raven undergoing winter overhaul on the slip at Waterside.

Right: Lady of the Lake, upon Ullswater at Glenridding in late 2010.

In 2010 on Ullswater the two grand old ladies, *Raven* and *Lady of the Lake* have been joined by three other smaller vessels. The average age of the vessels in fleet is 87 years old, surely making Ullswater home to one of the oldest fleets in the world.

In 2001 the Ullswater fleet saw a new addition arrive. *Lady Dorothy* was built in 1967 for service in the Channel Islands. Her main route was from St. Peter Port on Guernsey to Herm for Herm Seaways, a subsidiary of Trident Charter Company who operate the main fast ferries on the same route. She has a Perkins engine and this makes her capable of achieving 8 knots. She can carry up to 63 passengers. After her arrival in 2001 she was refurbished and painted in the house colours of green hull and white superstructure. *Lady Dorothy* has an open stern and a cabin from mid-ships right forward to the bow. She is shown here at Glenridding along with *Lady of the Lake*.

The arrival of *Lady Dorothy* meant that for the first time the company could offer a year round timetable. As she was built for service in the Channel Islands, *Lady Dorothy*'s hull was designed for rougher waters than the elegant lines of *Raven* and *Lady of the Lake* allowed. She commenced the first public sailings from Pooley Bridge in the winter of 2002/2003. *Lady Dorothy* is by far the smallest member of the Ullswater fleet and this means she is perfect for those days in winter when the weather beats outside, but the traveller is warm in the well-equipped saloon of the vessel. When the vessel is not needed for scheduled services she is often placed on a floating mooring in St. Patrick's Bay at the extreme southern end of the lake. She is approaching Pooley Bridge in this picture.

The first decade of the new millennium was one of great expansion for the Ullswater Navigation & Transit Company. After *Lady Dorothy* had settled in to service, the company looked at another new vessel and in 2005 *Lady Wakefield* joined the fleet. She had been built in 1949 for service on the River Dart and was named *Berry Castle* (III). In 1972 *Berry Castle* (III) was sold to a company who planned to use her as a dive boat but instead she moved on to Fareham and Rochester on the Medway and operated pleasure cruises under the name *Golden Cormorant*. She only lasted five years here and in 1977 she was to be found back on the River Dart. *Totnes Castle* is seen here on the right of this picture whilst working out of Totnes.

Her new owners, the Dart Pleasure Craft Company, renamed the vessel *Totnes Castle* (III) and used her for ferry duties and pleasure cruises from Plymouth. Plymouth Boat Cruises took over the services of the Dart Pleasure Craft Company in 1985 and operated *Totnes Castle* (III) until 2005 when she was sold for use on Ullswater. She was sailed up the coast to Whitehaven and from there she was moved on the back of a lorry to the lake. Her Gardner engines were refurbished in 2006, and she entered service the following year under her new name of *Lady Wakefield*. The new timetable for lake services reflected her arrival with even more services scheduled, including, for the first time, the possibility of a half lake cruise from Pooley Bridge which did not involve changing boats at Howtown. *Lady Wakefield* is at Pooley Bridge out of service for the winter in this picture.

Ullswater's newest addition is the *Western Belle*. Built in 1935 for the Millbrook Steam Boat & Trading Company. *Western Belle* was one of the incumbents on the Plymouth to Millbrook ferry until 1985 when the Millbrook Company stopped operating from Plymouth. She later served on the River Dart until 2000 when she moved to the River Thames where her owners were Chris Cruises of Hampton Court. She was sold to Ullswater in 2007. Her journey to the lake was quite an interesting one. To begin with she was sailed from the River Thames to Maryport, where she arrived in July 2008. She remained in Maryport until October when she travelled to the River Mersey to McTay's yard. This is a postcard of her when working for the Millbrook Steam Boat & Trading Company.

At McTay's yard *Western Belle* was to be overhauled before commencing service. She remained at the yard until July 2010 when she was moved by lorry to the lake, finally arriving in the evening of 13th July. She underwent final modifications on site before gaining her passenger certificate and entering service in late 2010. *Western Belle* is a larger vessel than *Lady Dorothy* and *Lady Wakefied*, but is smaller than *Raven* and *Lady of the Lake* and she brings the Ullswater fleet up to five. This picture shows *Western Belle* is at Glenridding during her first few weeks with a passenger certificate.